THE RELUCTANT REVOLUTIONARY

EDWARD TELLER, distinguished physicist, was concerned importantly with the planning and development of the atomic and hydrogen bombs, 1941-1951. Since 1953 he has been Professor of Physics at the University of California and is the author, with Francis O. Rice, of *The Structure of Matter* (1948); with A. L. Latter of *Our Nuclear Future* (1958); and with Alan Brown of *The Legacy of Hiroshima* (1962).

THE RELUCTANT REVOLUTIONARY

EDWARD TELLER

The Paul Anthony Brick Lectures
Third Series
1964

University of Missouri Press • Columbia

Library of Congress Catalog
Card Number 64-25274

Manufactured in the United States of America

Foreword

THE Paul Anthony Brick Lectureship Committee is pleased to present in the following pages the Third Series of lectures given at the University of Missouri under the Brick Fund. The Lectureship was opened in 1960 by three lectures on the topic, *Morals for Mankind*, given by Dr. Herbert W. Schneider. These were succeeded by a series presented in 1963 by Mr. Stringfellow Barr under the title, *The Three Worlds of Man.* Copies of both series of lectures are available from the University of Missouri Press.

The general purpose of the Lectureship is to make available to the reading public the conclusions of some of our most eminent authorities in the field of the application of ethics to some of our current social, cultural, scientific, and educational problems. According to the stipulations of the Lectureship the range of problems to be covered by the speakers has been purposely left broad in its sweep, and the individuals invited to participate have been freely allowed to select any ethical issues on which they felt they could make important contributions. The combination of unity and diversity which has been exhibited by the series thus far has amply justified the wisdom of this principle of selection.

The present series, given by the eminent physicist, Dr. Edward Teller, is devoted to some of the ethical problems which are faced by the scientist in carrying out his social responsibilities. Though Dr. Teller gave the lectures over a year ago (April 8, 9, 1963) he was unable because of the pressure of other work to which he had committed himself to revise them until recently into a form suitable for publication. It is perhaps noteworthy that in spite of two important changes in the world situation during this intervening period—the weakening of the cold war and the adoption of the test ban treaty—much of what Dr. Teller said on the occasion of the original lectures is still applicable today. Consequently the lectures as here published are substantially the same in content as those given in 1963.

However, they have been elaborately revised and rephrased by Dr. Teller in order to give them a form more suitable to the general reader.

A. Cornelius Benjamin
Chairman, Brick Committee

INTRODUCTION AND DEDICATION

THE following Brick Lectures delivered in 1963 at the University of Missouri form the basis of this little book. The passing months have not changed the essence of the ideas, but they have changed some of its applications. So what is now presented to the reader is a little different from what the audience heard.

The topic is the interaction of two different fields which have deeply moved the man of the twentieth century: science and politics. Both fields command respect; neither is easy. They are divergent—almost incompatible. Yet their joint influence will determine the attainment of our elementary needs and of our highest aims. The values and the ideals that the world will adopt are forged by the scientist and the politician.

In the first lecture, "The Noble Lie," I attempt to find the proper place of science and the scientist in the magnificent and troubled times in which we live. Plato has spoken about the rulers who are philosophers—or the philosophers who shall rule. Does the old wisdom of the *Republic* apply in our day?

In the second lecture, "Doomsday," the great change is discussed that first was brought to public attention at Hiroshima. There is no doubt that in the face of widespread confusion scientists must contribute to the public discussion. But when the scientists have made their contribution the common man will be left with questions, not with answers.

In the last lecture, "The Miracle of Freedom," I speak of the real core of our problem and of real solutions. But this difficult field I cannot enter as a scientist, only as one of the 180 million American citizens. The grave responsibility of our times no single group can rightly claim and no single individual may completely refuse. My hesitant answer to these questions has resulted in the title of this book: *The Reluctant Revolutionary.*

The danger of our time is human conflict. Science

changes the rules of conflict. Politics applies them. In a dangerous age our source of strength must be the guidance we take from each other. Therefore, it gives me a sense of reassurance to dedicate my efforts to three great men of Missouri whom I admire.

The first is former President Truman. His stature has grown with each passing year. His imaginative and courageous actions have saved freedom in Europe. It may be due to him that we still can shape our future.

The second is a man from whom I learned a little about politics: Senator Stuart Symington. If my knowledge remains limited, this is the fault of the pupil, not the master for whom I have a most sincere respect.

The third is a great scientist who worked for many years in Missouri: Arthur Holly Compton. No one has recognized more completely the responsibilities of a scientist. I should have liked to show him the manuscript of this book. Because of his untimely death his memory rather than his active advice must guide me.

Contents

I

THE NOBLE LIE

IT is hardly necessary to state that we are living in the age of science. All of us know that science produces change. This change means to some people hope, to others worry. It brings into our lives an adventure which may appear weird. On many of us it has placed a burden of responsibility for which we are not fully prepared. Science seems to have a different meaning for every individual.

My arguments will be related to science in a most intimate manner. There is no better way to introduce my subject than to describe a few facets of science that may be and a few that may not be uppermost in your minds.

The latest, most popular, most spectacular achievement of science is, of course, the conquest of space. Space travel used to be an impossible dream. Today it is a multibillion-dollar reality. Can any results ever justify such an extravagant undertaking?

I cannot give you any proof that our space effort is necessary. I happen to believe that the explorers of space will change the future of mankind, just as the navigators of the oceans changed our world five centuries ago. And as those sailors in their fragile vessels did not know toward what shores they were steering, so our astronauts today have no inkling what the impact of their remarkable experiences will be on our minds and our lives. None of us know.

But there are some results and some plans which I may mention. One cannot claim them as interest paid on our massive investment. One should regard them as symbols of things to come.

Our satellites watch the weather. Never before in history was it possible to know of rain and sunshine, heat and cold, breezes and hurricanes everywhere at the same time. A spacecraft completes its orbit in ninety minutes, collects all relevant data and feeds them into big and stupid machines, computers, which cannot remember as much as one-millionth of what a freshman knows. But the computer can do something with what we have put into its memory at a rate a hundred thousand times faster than the speed with which your professors claim to think. And with the help of these machines we have good hopes that in an hour's time we shall project weather twenty-four hours ahead. We shall yet make an honest man of the weather prophet. Having found the causes of weather, we might find means to influence it. And when we have done that, something terrible will have happened: We will have lost the last safe topic of conversation. There will be Republican rainstorms and Democratic droughts, and the climate of Siberia will have become a trick of the dirty capitalists. The practical knowledge we shall find in our Promethean quest will give us even more power together with its inseparable companions: the highest of hopes and the gravest of perils.

But let me turn away from the practical aspects. Let me say something that you may know but that you may not fully remember and that may not appear to you in correct proportions. We talk about the travel to the stars. Do you know what we are talking about? Do you know how far the stars are? By the end of the century we probably shall have explored our planetary system. But once that is done the next fixed star, Alpha Centauri, is four light-years away. And the most effective rocket, propelled by the same fuel that is used in the hydrogen bombs, will probably take at least a hundred years to get there.

What about exploring even more distant places? We are living in an assembly of hundred billion stars, the Milky Way System. The Milky Way has a core; you may call it a metropolitan area where stars are close enough for interstellar commerce, war, or cultural exchange. This assembly of brilliant stars is hidden from us by a cloud of dust. If we could see it, it would appear one-tenth as bright as the full moon.

But we are living in a Godforsaken neck of the woods. Even the light of our sun takes thirty thousand years if it wants to get "downtown." An astronaut would take much longer. In our corner of the universe habitable planetary systems are separated by distances that no future Niña, Pinta, or Santa Maria can easily bestride.

Still, I have not yet told you how big space is: Space is much bigger. Next to our own Milky Way System there is another one, the Andromeda Nebula. The word "next" means that Andromeda is two million light-years away. And then, million light-year by million light-year (and light, you know, can go as fast as anything can go) we see more of these assemblies of a hundred billion stars, with their countless planetary systems never to be seen by our feeble instruments. And in these billions upon billions of little worlds there may be found things stranger than life.

You may also know that even now we see these galaxies following each other out to distances of more than a billion light-years. Soon we may be able to see a place so far away that when light left it, the universe may have been young. We might yet find out about the act of creation if indeed the inquiry about creation makes any sense. One is reminded of the words of Isaac Newton, who first made our world small and our universe big. He described himself as a child playing with pretty pebbles on the shores of the great ocean of knowledge. The ocean which now lies before us is space. We may never cross it.

But we may learn something about it. We indeed have already learned something which to us scientists appears more impressive than size and more remarkable than any practical application. We have learned that space and time are not the clean, simple, comfortable apriori-given filing systems that philosophers imagined them to be. Most particularly time is not the simple orderly flow of events that any child can understand. We used to believe that two events are either simultaneous, or one has occurred earlier than the other. In common experiment this decision can be made without difficulty. But if you talk about an event today on the Andromeda Nebula, the earliest time you can find out about it is in two million years. And if you ask what happened first, the conquest of Gaul by Julius Caesar or the explosion of a star in a nearby galaxy, the signal of which is not going to arrive for much more than a million years, we are indeed faced with a puzzle. We have learned from Einstein the apparently nonsensical fact that the question which of these events has occurred earlier not only cannot be easily determined, but in fact will depend on the speed with which the observer is traveling. Different observers will find that the time sequence of the events is different—and each of them is right from his point of view. A door has opened into a new kind of thinking—not, as is generally believed, a more complicated kind of thinking, but to a way of looking at the world which is simple, but is so surprising, so strongly opposed to common sense, that most people react to it with the emotional statement, "I do not understand." What this statement really means: "It's so crazy that I won't listen to it."

A short time ago I gave a course of elementary lectures to freshmen. My son was one of the students. After I had described the new facts of Einstein's relativity, he whispered to his neighbor, a fellow-student,

"Do you believe what he says?" The boy answered: "Not really, but I don't think he is to be blamed for it."

Let us turn from the overwhelming, disorderly world of stars (which merits the name of chaos much more than that of cosmos) to the miniature, neat miracles of unimaginable precision, the atoms. Here the scientists have found lessons even more surprising than the paradoxes of Einstein. An understanding of atomic physics had to be bought by sacrificing the oldest postulate of science: causality. No longer need we accept the stanza of Omar Khayyám:

> And that inverted Bowl they call the Sky,
> Whereunder crawling cooped we live and die,
> Lift not your hands to *It* for help—for It
> As impotently moves as you or I.

The strange fact is that atoms are not impotent, predetermined, machine-like objects. They are orderly and at the same time unpredictable entities like "you or I." Whether they will help us, of course, will depend on ourselves.

In any case practical applications of the newly found atomic knowledge abound. Let us start with an example that is important for the more graceful half of our race: nylons. Having explored the structure of the molecule, it was possible to use atomic architecture to the extent that in a cheap and synthetic manner it was possible to produce something more practical, more pretty, more useable, more saleable, than the products of the ancient butterflies that lived on the Chinese mulberry trees. But when the chemists first succeeded in producing the new silk of science, it was not put on the market for feminine hosiery. It was used for parachutes in World War II. Can one ever tell whether a new invention will satisfy a need, cater to a luxury, or become a weapon?

Let us turn to another example: Some historians still talk about the Stone Age, the Copper Age, the Bronze Age, and the Iron Age. They do not mention the fact that the Iron Age is at an end. In more and more applications we are replacing iron by aluminum and other new metals. We have understood the connections between chemistry and physics in real detail, and this makes it possible to overturn whole industries, to change economic conditions. Indeed we no longer live in the Iron Age, but in the Scientific Age, in which atoms, electricity, and even empty space do our bidding.

Let me turn to one more topic: biology, the science of life. I do not know what I am. But I do know that I consist of a little amount of matter and an enormous amount of complication. The chemists, in a most disquieting manner, are beginning to untangle this complication. The result may depart from traditional common sense even more radically than relativity or the theory of the atom. And in the riddle of life there is contained an even more disturbing question: What is consciousness? Yet, one has the feeling that we might, we just might, begin to understand something about these problems. And I will make one bet, that if we find an answer, it will not fit in anybody's philosophy. It will not look like anybody's predictions or dreams and will not have been approached by the many uncontrolled phantasies of the science-fiction writers. Science has proved again and again that facts are very much stranger than anything our imagination can invent.

This is the scene. Our life has changed. Our philosophy has every reason to change. But while we have acquired the fruit of knowledge, we have started to notice that it has a bitter taste. It is the most common observation to say that the rapid advancement of science has made our small globe an extremely dangerous place in which to live. And who has done it? Of course, the scientists. They should now find the means to rescue us from our superabundance of power. This is their moral responsibility, isn't it? Furthermore, science has become too complicated; knowledge is advancing too rapidly. The layman can hardly understand the new problems and can certainly not solve them. Better leave it all to the scientists.

I have made the last statements with some hesitation. But I could not avoid them. Ideas of this kind are often implied and quite a few times they are brought out boldly into open discussion. What is, indeed, the responsibility of a scientist? How are his activities related to the most concrete and most horrible danger that faces us, the possibility of a third World War?

The common answer is that the scientist is indeed responsible for the fruit of his labor. It is one of my main objectives to question this conclusion. We are obviously dealing with a problem of responsibility and morality. We can discuss; we cannot present a proof. But discussion may lead to a different point of view, a new insight, perhaps even to deeply felt conviction. At the very least, discussion should guard us against the blind acceptance of widespread but superficial beliefs.

As a result of a new public acceptance of scientific authority in politics, important changes are occurring in our government. It is a fact that today among the group of most influential people in Washington, 10 or 20 per cent are scientists. There is no question but that the scientists are very heavily over-represented. This is not surprising. When the scientists were told that they are responsible their moral feelings rose to the occasion. When they were told that they are the only ones clever enough to accept the heavy burden there was hardly a whisper of protest.

This kind of thinking is not new. Socrates has been talking about it and the scientists in turn have been reading Socrates. In Plato's *Republic* in which Socrates expounds his ideas about how an ideal community should be governed, it is proposed that all power should be exercised by a small number of guardians. These men should receive a most rigorous education. They shall own no property, devote all their lives to the commonwealth, live together as in a military camp, and having proved during many years of apprenticeship that they are strong, wise, and unselfish, they should take over the unchecked, unbalanced direction of the state. In the common language, these highly educated, highly dedicated people, have been usually described as *philosopher kings*. Plato calls them *guardians*. Do they not bear some resemblance to our idea of a *scientist?*

I have read the *Republic*[1] carefully and I have stumbled over some passages. We know that democracy is good; Plato, we are told, is excellent. The two must agree. Do they? Let us look at some passages:

> if we intend our citizens to be brave, must we not add to this such lessons as are likely to preserve them most

[1]The selections are from *The Republic of Plato,* translated into English by John Llewelyn Davies and David James Vaughan (London: Macmillan & Co., Ltd., 1921).

> effectually from being afraid of death? or do you think a man can ever become brave who is haunted by the fear of death?
>
> No, indeed, I do not.
>
> Well, do you imagine that a believer in Hades and its terrors will be free from all fear of death, and in the day of battle will prefer it to defeat and slavery?
>
> Certainly not. . . .
>
> Then we shall expunge [does that sound like censorship?] the following passage, and with it all that are like it.

The passage to be censored is from Homer.

> "And those chambers be seen both by mortal men and immortals,
> Terrible, dank, and mouldering,—even to gods an abhorrence."[2]

You must not read this, even though in Greek and even in English it sounds well. Then again,

> Our guardians ought not be given to laughter, for when any one indulges in violent laughter, such excess almost universally invites an equally violent reaction. . . . Then if a poet represents even men of any consideration as overcome by laughter, our approval must be withheld; much more if gods are so described. . . . That being the case, we shall not allow Homer to speak of the gods in such terms as the following:
>
> "Straight 'mid the blessed gods brake forth unquenchable laughter,
> When they beheld Hephaestus go bustling from chamber to chamber."[3]

[2]*Ibid.*, iii. 386.
[3]*Ibid.*, iii. 389.

Censorship is not practiced in a democratic country. Plato's *Republic* seems to resemble a dictatorship.

And here comes a passage, which to me is particularly interesting.

> To the rulers of the state . . . it belongs of right to use falsehood, to deceive either enemies or their own citizens, for the good of the state: and no one else may meddle with this privilege.[4]

That is the practical thing to do. It seems that the Russians have negotiated with us for a year about a test ban, while they have been preparing to violate this ban in a very effective manner. They must have read Plato.

There are many examples of the absolute power of the guardians in the *Republic.* Plato asks whether we ought

> to confine ourselves to superintending our poets, and compelling them to impress on their productions the likeness of a good moral character, on pain of not composing among us; or ought we to extend our superintendence to the professors of every other craft as well?[5]

The answer turns out to be yes. The suggestion of using falsehood for the good of the state, the very thing which has been designed as the "Noble Lie," is explained at least in one case in a little detail:

---

[4]*Ibid.*, iii. 389.
[5]*Ibid.*, iii. 401.

> can we contrive any ingenious mode of bringing into play one of those seasonable falsehoods of which we lately spoke, so that, propounding a single spirited fiction, we may bring even the rulers themselves, if possible to believe it . . . ?[6]

It is a most remarkable thing, to lie so effectively that you believe it yourself.

> We shall tell our people, in mythical language: You are doubtless all brethren, as many as inhabit the city, but the God who created you mixed gold in the composition of such of you as are qualified to rule, which gives them the highest value; while the auxiliaries he made silver an ingredient, assigning iron and copper to the cultivators of the soil and the other workmen.[7]

This is the noble lie. And let us ask about the golden guardians:

> will these guardians be the smallest of all the classes . . . ?
>
> Yes, much the smallest.
>
> Then it is the knowledge residing in its smallest class or section, that is to say, in the predominant and ruling body, which entitles a state, organized agreeably to nature, to be called wise as a whole; and that class whose right and duty it is to partake of the knowledge which alone of all kinds of knowledge is properly called wisdom, is naturally, as it appears, the least numerous body in the state.[8]

That is the government by the philosopher kings. This may become the government of the scientists, if ever the modern *Republic* should be realized.

---

[6]*Ibid.*, iii. 414.
[7]*Ibid.*, iii. 415.
[8]*Ibid.*, iii. 429.

And what about democracy? As compared to the wise rule by a small and highly disciplined body of men who have devoted all their lives to the art of ruling, Plato says about democracy:

> this constitution may be the most beautiful of all. Embroidered as it is with every kind of character it may be thought as beautiful as a coloured dress, embroidered with every kind of flower. And perhaps, I added, as children and women admire dresses of many colours, so many persons will decide in favor of this commonwealth, as the most beautiful.[9]

For women and children! And as to the man who lives in this society, the democratic man:

> whenever he is told that though some pleasure belong to the appetites which are good and honourable, others belong to the evil appetites; and that the former ought to be practised and respected, but the latter chastised and enslaved, he does not receive this true doctrine, or admit it into his castle. On the contrary, at all these assertions he shakes his head, and maintains that all appetites are alike and ought to be equally respected. . . .
>
> Hence . . . he lives from day to day to the end in the gratification of the casual appetite,—now drinking himself drunk to the sound of music and presently putting himself under training;—sometimes idling and neglecting everything, and then living like a student of philosophy. And often he takes a part in public affairs, and starting up, speaks and acts according to the impulse of the moment. Now he follows eagerly

[9] *Ibid.*, viii. 557.

> in the steps of certain great generals, because he covets their distinctions; and anon he takes to trade, because he envies the successful trader. And there is no order or constraining rule in his life; but he calls this life of his, pleasant, and liberal, and happy, and follows it out to the end.[10]

It is clear: Plato holds democracy in low esteem.

There is a very serious point in all of this. If, indeed, we delegate authority over essential things to a small body of men, we have betrayed the simplest principles of democracy. Any small governing group, whether they be scientists or philosophers, kings or generals, communists or fascists, aristocrats or even gangsters, will govern in an autocratic manner. This is a basic fact. Firm opposition to autocracy, to the government of the few, is the basic fact of democracy. In some instances the few have governed in the best interest of all. But on the whole, the story of mankind has shown that rule by a minority is very good for that minority. For the majority it is not so good.

Is there indeed any sense in the argument that the scientist should make the decisions? Is it true that because a scientist has conceived the atom and has put it to use he should now say what to do with it? Do we insist that the men who make the laws, the legislators, should apply these laws? Or do we rather

[10] *Ibid.*, viii. 561.

separate the powers of the congress from that of the judges? Do we insist that our generals who know most about war should make the decisions between peace and war? Rightly or wrongly, in a democracy we say that powers should be divided, and the ultimate power must belong to the people.

It is possible for the layman to make the decisions in the bewildering years of technological and scientific revolution? I say it is. Science today is simple. It is easier to learn than it was a hundred years ago. True, the facts are more numerous, but the system embracing all of these facts is much more complete, unified, and therefore easier to understand. He who takes the trouble to get acquainted with the strange ideas of science can put himself into the position of knowing his way around in science, of having an ear for science, as many of us have an ear for music. It is possible for the educated layman to distinguish correct statements from nonsense, once the facts are stated, explained, and discussed.

After all, returning to the question of weapons, for instance, if a weapon is perfected, its effects, its consequences, are easily understood and easily explained. This understanding and explanation is to some extent impeded by our practice of secrecy. Sometimes I suspect that the secrecy itself is due to a public refusal of responsibility. The common man seems ready to abdicate his democratic responsibility. I deeply believe that not to practice democracy, to leave decisions to the scientist, is dangerous. I believe that it is dangerous for our country and that it is dangerous for science.

It is dangerous for our country because scientists have been trained in a peculiar manner. They are faced with surprising and sharply defined situations; they deal with puzzles which are like chess problems. With all elements in their hands, they make a choice; it might be very difficult but it can be done, and once the solution is found there is no doubt about it.

The political decisions call for entirely different abilities. They call for an understanding of a great number of facts. They call for decisions made on the basis of insufficient evidence. More than anything, politics calls for feeling and compromise—things that the scientist in his narrow field has no occasion to practice. When he deals with the magnificent web of nature he may be a genius; in the ever-changing world of human relations he often is a child.

But government by scientists is not only a danger to the country; it is also a danger to science. Scientists have all too frequently given wrong advice in the past. Society might turn against them and may accuse them not only of misjudgment but, indeed, of conspiracy with dictatorial intentions. Of course, there is no such conspiracy. No matter what I have said about Plato's *Republic*, what is happening is not due to intent, it is due to the force of circumstances.

If public resentment should be aroused against the scientists this will be bad enough. What scientists do to themselves is worse. Being considered wise and incomprehensible, scientists are losing the habit of clear and simple expression. In the last century Faraday explained his revolutionary experiments and theories in simple lectures, aimed at teen-agers. This style is going out of practice. And the scientists who are no longer making an attempt to talk the universal language of the public have even started to lose touch with each other. Science is atomized, and each of us when talking about science is living in his own ivory tower. We talk in polysyllables and we converse only with our closest associates. Sometimes we notice that nobody understands us but ourselves.

There is, however, a real responsibility for scientists and this responsibility is great. The scientist's responsibility is to find out what he can about nature. It is his responsibility to use new knowledge to extend man's power over nature. He is the creator of new tools, more fantastic than those described in the tales of the thousand-and-one nights of Arabia.

When the scientist has learned what he can learn and when he has built what he is able to build his work is not yet done. He must also explain in clear, simple, and understandable terms what he has found and what he has constructed. And there his responsibility ends. The decision on how to use the results of science is not his. The right and the duty to make decisions belongs to the people.

I believe that the scientist's responsibility is limited. By being limited it is actually more difficult. What he has to do no one else can do in his stead. And the last of his jobs, to explain clearly and objectively his results, may well turn out to be superhuman. Who can be objective? Who can separate undeniable facts from implied conclusions? Let us not expect too much from scientific objectivity. Let us be content if the scientist attempts to be honest. Let us not assume that he is unprejudiced. But let us require that he name his prejudices. Free debate between prejudiced advocates is a tortuous road toward truth. But it has proved more reliable than any straight doctrine.

The scientist has done his full duty only if he becomes a full participant of our vital, paradoxical, multicolored, democratic society. Our society is "embroidered with every kind of flower" and of these flowers science is one of the most beautiful. Its beauty is indeed due to a constraining rule (which Plato denies to the democrat), but this rule is not possession of truth, not authority based on truth, but rather endless search for truth and continued sharing of every new truth and every new problem with our fellow-citizens.

I have talked today about science and about scientists. And on some occasions I have used the weapons of ridicule. I am acutely aware of the fact that I am ridiculing myself. Nevertheless, I want you to know that there is nothing which I would put higher than science. By this I do not claim any fraction of the pre-eminence of the guardians, because in human life and particularly in the life of a democracy there are and there should be many highest points. For the mountain climber, the conquest of the summit is the only real passion. For the musician (and I have a little understanding for him), there cannot exist anything even vaguely comparable to the magnificence of music. The tiller of the soil feels it in his bones that everything starts and ends in the good earth. To the physician there cannot be any more exalted profession than to give health and life. A dedicated politician is deeply aware of the fact that he is carrying a superhuman responsibility on his all-too-human shoulders, and this knowledge gives him courage and strength. In our world there are and there must be many perfections.

The perfection of science has a special role, because our age is the age of science. It is science that changes our lives, our habits, our hopes, and our fears from decade to decade. Science is the motor which propels us with increasing speed into an uncertain future. And at the same time science is the system of learning that opens up before us thoughts, ideas, that nobody ever has dreamed before. Only by the proper concentration on his great task can the scientist perform the difficult and wonderful job that could and should be his.

II

DOOMSDAY

IN the summer of 1945, World War II came to a sudden end. So did the isolation and the safety of the United States. It became clear that disastrous weapons of the future can be delivered without warning. In the intervening years, this situation became even more acute and menacing. We now know that a rocket will take but twenty minutes to span the ocean and deliver its devastating burden upon a military, industrial, or urban target.

In the long history of the United States, our country has enjoyed a great amount of safety. And the people of the United States have made good use of the safety and of the peace. The United States had to participate in the dreadful wars of the twentieth century, but it did not have to prepare ahead of time. We could watch and see the danger rising, then still make our contribution in such a way that America itself was not touched by the fury of war.

For the first time in more than a century our frontiers are open to aggression. Past generations were sheltered; we find ourselves exposed in a hazardous world, and there is among us a great feeling of anxiety. Anxiety has a remarkable nature. It is disturbing and very often, particularly in this case, it may turn into unconstructive channels. The fear of a catastrophe is particularly disturbing because what we are afraid of is something without precedent, is something that we cannot imagine and something against which for these very reasons it is difficult to make realistic preparations. What is happening is something that from a logical point of view we must consider strange. But from the point of view of the psychologist, from the point of view of the man who knows the human soul, what is happening is probably just what should be expected.

If you are worried about something that is not before your eyes, about something which you cannot measure, estimate, or even imagine, the most usual and the easiest thing to do is to forget about it and not to do anything. Then, having forgotten about it and having not quite forgotten about it, you turn around and talk about these dangers in a way that exaggerates the dangers. What the conscious mind has decided to disregard visits you in your dreams.

We have been told again and again that there is no defense, that indeed the world, the human race, and most certainly any form of civilization will necessarily come to an end, once an all-out atomic war should break out. This is a most difficult situation. It is full of ambiguity, even for those who happen to know something about the actual nature of what might happen. There is no doubt that if nuclear war ever should be the misfortune of the world, and the misfortune of ourselves, such a war will be unprecedented in its suddenness and its fury. No war of the past has been ever realistically predicted. And it would be foolhardy to try to describe and to predict what would happen in a nuclear conflict. When the nuclear bomb was developed, when people saw its effect one thousand times as great as the biggest explosive used in World War II, it was called the absolute weapon, the weapon to end all weapons. Then a few years later something else was developed which was a thousand times bigger still.

Where is all this going to lead? It seems indeed to be the end of the world; and if the human race is faced with the probability of extinction, our conventional way of thinking surely can no longer be valid. You can hardly open a book these days, hardly participate in a serious conversation, without this awful prospect popping up in one form or another—if not explicitly, at least by a hint. And yet, we are not doing anything to defend ourselves, because we have been told, and we are deeply convinced, that there is no place to hide, that there is no defense against the absolute weapon. If there should be any more proof required that what I have said is indeed so, I only have to quote from the brilliant inauguration address of a great President of these United States. In January, 1961, President Kennedy used this sentence, "Man holds in his mortal hand the power to destroy all forms of human life." Can one wonder that under these conditions thoughtful people with good reason do raise the question: Is it better to be Red or dead?

Now here is the point that I would like to make. The statement of President Kennedy, which I have just quoted, was based on faulty information. There is no concrete way in which human life is apt to be ended on our planet, none that we know about, none that I can think about. All that I have told you in the last paragraphs, all that I have mentioned about the doomsday of the human race is based on unrealistic generalities. I talked to one of my friends who has discussed with seemingly scientific thoroughness the "doomsday bomb." I asked him whether he knew a way in which to produce such an instrument. He answered: "No, but you cannot prove that such a weapon can never be made." The imagination of man knows no limits and it often is attracted by cataclysmic visions.

In my first lecture I talked about the responsibility of the scientist. I attempted to convince you that it is not the responsibility of the scientist to participate in an essential fashion in our government in a policy-making capacity. The responsibility of the scientist is to find what he can, understand nature, and use his knowledge to create new tools for all of us. Then he should explain as clearly as possible, as precisely as can be, what he has found, and what he has done. In our present grave situation it should be the responsibility of the scientist to say in clear and explicit language what is the actual danger of an atomic conflict. Is it true that atomic war would be the end of our race? The danger has been exaggerated. My purpose and my duty is to set the record straight.

When people talk about the end of the human race, there is one specific danger that the speaker and his audience have in mind. This danger is radioactive fallout. We have been told that even the testing of nuclear weapons is dangerous. If, then, instead of testing, those nuclear weapons should be exploded many thousand times, then indeed it is plausible that the whole human race should be subjected to deadly radiation. You may have read the book or seen the movie, "On the Beach," and this masterfully written piece of literature has surely convinced many of you that the danger is real.

Before I go any further, I would like to make one clear and simple statement. A nuclear attack on the United States, no matter how we defend ourselves against it, will be a very terrible thing. To take this possibility lightly is complete madness. But there is a difference between an unprecedented disaster and the end of the human race. Specifically, the question of radiation is something that we know about. We can evaluate its consequences simply, completely, and quantitatively. Testing has led to a level of radiation which amounts to no more than a few per cent of natural radiation. This is a situation very different from the alarming picture that the press and the fallout propaganda have conjured up in the public mind. Still the facts are indubitable. Fallout is only a few per cent of the natural background. Furthermore, natural radiation is much older than the human race and it has effects exceedingly similar to fallout. In my opinion one cannot speak properly of a danger of worldwide fallout due to testing.

In a nuclear conflict, very much greater amounts of radiation can be produced, and it is probable that in an all-out nuclear war the United States, if it is bombed, will be subjected to heavy doses of radiation which will kill many people—how many depend on the circumstances. It will particularly depend on the question of whether or not we have properly prepared our defenses.

If we turn to the worldwide effect of all these weapons we can say on the basis of the experience of our testing rather precisely what the effects of widespread radiation would be. Since the argument of worldwide destruction has been raised I must discuss amounts of radioactivity which, indeed, would have a worldwide effect. Consider the case that ten thousand times as much radioactivity should be released into the air as has been produced by all past tests. This would amount to nuclear weapons with a total yield of three, four, five million megatons, an almost inconceivable amount of destructive power. It is much more than any military plan would call for. To talk of such an amount of radioactivity is unrealistic. Let us assume, however, that it should be released and distributed around the earth. It would indeed seriously affect everyone. But even assuming that no one takes any measures to defend himself, it still would not destroy humanity. It would increase the natural rate of mutation a few-fold, and this indeed would be a further reason for worry. But these mutations would not bring about the end of mankind. And further, if proper and possible countermeasures are taken, like cleaning of food supplies, trying to avoid contaminated places, the damage could be held to a small fraction of the destruction that an all-out war would necessarily produce.

I have talked about a truly dreadful amount of nuclear explosives. In Congressional hearings there have been discussions of possible attacks on the United States. In those discussions there is envisaged approximately 1 per cent of the explosive power that I have mentioned to you. And that 1 per cent, it is claimed, and rightly claimed, would be under present circumstances enough to destroy our country.

The amount of explosives that I have mentioned—three or four or five million megatons—would be equivalent to the delivery of one Hiroshima-type weapon on every square mile of our globe, every square mile, whether land, sea, mountain, or arctic waste. If ever anyone would want to do something comparable to that, the damage by the shock, by the fires, by the immediate action of the weapons would be incomparably greater than the damage caused by worldwide fallout.

You may ask, aren't there other weapons that could endanger mankind? What about the famous cobalt bomb? The cobalt bomb exists only in the imagination of people who want to scare us. It could be made, but in a military sense it would be completely useless. The cobalt bomb is designed to do little damage to military targets but to kill the greatest number of people all over the globe. No aggressor would want to do that: to leave his enemy relatively undamaged, but instead to wreak disaster upon as many neutral people (and upon himself) as he possibly could. Even if somebody would use these cobalt bombs, and even if no countermeasures were taken, if one would let the cobalt sift down to the surface of the earth and leave it there where it could do most damage, even then the danger would be only three or four times as great as that due to more conventional bombs. But to clean up these amounts that actually descend upon the surface of the earth is relatively easy—particularly so because the action of the cobalt is slow; it extends over five years. It would be more difficult to deal with the cobalt if it should stay in the atmosphere where one cannot clean it up; but in that case we are exposed only to a small fraction of the cobalt radiation and then the danger is much smaller than the danger from normal fission bombs.

The actual trend in the explosive development is quite different from the one discussed in the last paragraphs. Each year our bombs are getting cleaner and cleaner. This trend is due to a variety of reasons. We work on clean nuclear explosives because we hope to use them for peaceful purposes. But we also work on them because any responsible military person will prefer a clean weapon to a dirty one. A clean weapon does damage by shock, or other means, at the place where the damage is intended. A dirty weapon, in addition, produces radioactivity carried by the wind to unpredictable places, where it does damage at random, where it will kill indiscriminately noncombatants, neutrals, friends, and foes alike. The development has been clearly and increasingly toward clean nuclear explosives. There is no reason to believe that radiation will be the end of mankind.

There is, however, a simpler worry. Nuclear weapons have grown bigger and more devastating. Is it not predictable that they will continue to grow and eventually destroy their makers together with all other men?

One must admit that the future is uncertain. One must recognize that human power is frightening. But each increase in our ability to do damage was the result of a difficult and expensive development. In each case the development was motivated by military need. Military requirements continue to stimulate research on weapons. But these requirements no longer demand bigger weapons. There is agreement on this point: Our weapons are big enough.

What we need today is smaller weapons, more flexible weapons, above all, weapons of defense. The popular phrase "overkill" does apply to the size of some nuclear explosions which played a great role in propaganda and pseudoscientific writing. The real effort in our country and I believe also in Russia is not directed toward useless size but toward the realistic questions of how to destroy the enemy's military potential and how to save one's own people and one's own power. A doomsday bomb might be constructed, made with a gigantic effort of ingenuity, organization, and resources. But there is no human society that is going to work on this enterprise even if it were feasible.

Of course, we have even today enough nuclear explosives to destroy cities and peoples in a most dreadful manner. But this is not new. Read the sad annals of war and you will find that the worst in the past was just as bad as the worst we may expect in the future. This is no consolation because the worst in the past was terrible indeed. But we should not consider ourselves in a unique and unprecedented position. Let me remind you of one of the most terrible wars. In the year 1220 Genghis Khan invaded Persia. He was far removed from his base. He made up his mind that in order to subdue Persia he must destroy it. He must leave nobody alive. And this is what he did. The Mongols would ride into a city and kill every man, woman, and child, except those who had crawled away and hidden. Then the Mongols would leave, and the people who saved themselves would emerge from their hiding places. In three days the Mongols would return and kill everybody whom they could find. It is estimated, and I don't know how accurately, that in that dreadful war more than 90 per cent of the Persians were killed. Persia used to be a great, flourishing country; it never recovered. Nuclear war, if it ever comes, may well be as terrible as that, for the country that is attacked. It is a fearful fact that such horrors are not new. Ever since man has gained power over the forces of nature, ever since he found out how to fashion weapons, the amount of damage that he did was not limited by anything except his own decision. The danger is Man. Nothing can save us except the powers of reason and morality in Man himself.

This is a dreadful topic; but because it has been discussed in such detail in the past, I have to stay with it a while longer. I don't like to talk about it and you don't like to listen, but it is better to know than to have the anxiety of an ill-defined dream. Open discussion is certainly preferable to the Noble Lie of Plato's *Guardians.* We cannot be satisfied if we are given well-intentioned programs based on misleading statements. If there is any question in which all of us must know the basic facts, it is the question of survival.

We must have a clear understanding whether it is possible that these dreadful amounts of nuclear explosives will ever rain down on the surface of the earth. Linus Pauling has estimated in several speeches that our stockpile today is approximately one-tenth of what I have described to you, one-tenth of the amount that would very seriously jeopardize a great number of people, but would certainly not end the human race. He has further estimated that the number and destructive power of these weapons will continue to grow rapidly. The statements of Linus Pauling on this particular subject are based on precisely no information. Why does he make these statements? I don't want to accuse him of telling us something of which he cannot be certain. I would rather accuse myself and accuse many in the government for failing to contradict Linus Pauling's statements in a clear, complete, and quantitative manner. Unfortunately, I cannot contradict him, because the number of nuclear weapons we possess is a secret. I may not tell you this number, but I have a very good guess that the Russians know it. We have arrived at a stage where the democratic process cannot function. The common man, the voter who should make the decisions, can be scared by unproven statements, and these statements cannot be authoritatively contradicted on account of secrecy. Using published testimony before Congressional committees I can at least say that very much smaller amounts of explosives are sufficient to wreck those targets which one can expect to destroy by nuclear explosives.

Any plan of attack or defense will be satisfied with a small fraction of the explosives that I have mentioned. Any wartime objective that can be accomplished at all can be accomplished with fewer bombs. The military people, in Russia, in this country, and everywhere else, will not invest their effort in a senseless over-production of nuclear explosives. Rather they will use their money and their effort in delivery systems, in systems for defense, in a multitude of detailed and difficult technological measures which will allow them to deliver their explosives at those places where they count most.

I conclude, and I conclude with complete confidence, that as far as one can foresee today, the human race will not come to an end. And the end of the world is not any closer than it was in the year of 999 when people for entirely different reasons imagined that the millenium would see the end of earthly existence. But if that is good news, I will have to temper it with some very bad news indeed. The world will not come to an end. If we do not look out the United States will. A small fraction of the force that I have described to you, an amount of power which probably is available today in Russia and which now or in the near future will be ready for delivery, can wipe out the United States beyond any hope of recovery. We will probably be able to strike back and will be able to do similar damage to Russia. Because of this fact of deterrence it is likely that the Russians will actually not wipe us out, as long as they don't find means of parrying our retaliation blow. Will they find an effective defense? If so, they may be ready to strike. The danger is great and the danger is acute. And I would like to add, I *have* to add, the danger is to a great extent unnecessary. The fact is that there *is* a possibility to defend ourselves against an atomic attack.

Let me talk for a while about defense. It is a question of the greatest possible public importance. First of all, it is possible to shoot down nuclear explosives, even when delivered with the help of missiles. These missiles move much faster than a bullet, but they can be tracked and they can be shot down with very effective, yet small and clean nuclear explosives. A complete defense is not likely to be invented, for a very simple reason. If the Russians should hurl against us thousands of missiles, they are likely to accompany this swarm of nuclear explosives by decoys. The number of the decoys can and probably will be so great that it will be impossible to shoot down every missile and every decoy. It is difficult, but fortunately it is possible, to distinguish between the missiles and the decoys. It is possible because a decoy can be delivered cheaply only when it is light. But if the decoy has little weight it will be easily stopped as soon as it begins to penetrate the atmosphere. The atmosphere is a protective layer, and as the decoys and the bombs enter the atmosphere we can find out which is which. Then we can shoot, but then it is too late; because by that time the bombs are close enough to destroy our cities.

Does this mean that missile defense is useless? If you think in very simple terms, you may now declare that missile defense is a waste of effort. In fact, however, another answer is possible. If you shoot down the missiles before they touch the ground and if you force the attacker to detonate his bombs at high altitudes the effects of the explosions will have changed in two important respects: No deadly concentrations of radioactivity will be deposited and the direct effects of the explosions will be decreased. The result of the nuclear attack will still be terrible. But there will be significant differences which must be understood.

If a nuclear bomb explodes near the ground a great deal of dust and debris is stirred up. Radioactive atoms attach themselves to this dust. Within one mile, ten miles, or one hundred miles in the downwind direction the contaminated dust settles and produces enough radiation to give a deadly dose to anyone outside a radiation shelter. Radioactivity from bombs bursting on the ground may become the most widespread killer in a nuclear attack. Missile defense would greatly reduce this particular danger because high-altitude explosions do not stir up any dust. Radioactivity from such explosions rises into the stratosphere. It spreads, it gets diluted, the most fierce activities decay and only after all this has happened does the activity settle down to the earth's surface. By that time the activity has spread over oceans and continents. In wars, as we can foresee them, this activity will no longer do grave damage to human life.

It is harder to get rid of the direct effects of nuclear bombs. The explosion sends out a shock wave which knocks down buildings. In the rubble, fires spring up.

The incandescent explosion itself sends out heat-rays which ignite some materials even beyond the destructive range of the shock. It is probable that high-altitude explosions will produce all this damage if the attacking bombs are big enough.

But while we cannot save our cities, we can save our people. We can build the proper kind of shelters and we can build them so that the shelters and everybody who is in the shelters will be safe against the bombs that have not touched the ground but have been exploded reasonably high in the atmosphere.

What will such a shelter program cost? This has been studied. In many regions where the ground is dry and does not consist of the hardest rocks, a satisfactory shelter will cost $200 per person. For a few per cent of our military expenditures we could provide very many of our endangered citizens with a shelter. Further plans could be developed which could give protection to everyone. We could develop, and to some extent we have developed, a system of warning. If the shelters are so distributed that you can get into them, having walked five or ten minutes, the great majority of our people will be safe. These shelters will give complete protection against fallout. They will be safe against any kind of a fire and they can be so built that they will stand up to a megaton explosion if it is no closer than a mile. They will survive a hundred megaton explosion if it is no closer than four miles. Proper missile defense can make sure that no nuclear bomb gets that close to our cities.

There is no doubt that if we are suddenly attacked, there will be many who won't find shelter. It is obvious that in a nuclear war there will be more than one attack. And it is clear that there will be millions upon millions of casualties. But the bulk of our people, 90 per cent of our people, could and must survive. If such an attack ever comes (and it need not come and should not come), and if we were properly prepared, still many individuals would die; but the nation can survive.

We have not made these preparations. So far we have spent something like one-tenth of 1 per cent of all our military expenditures on civil defense. So far we have not exercised the art of pure and peaceful self-protection. Why not? Out of laxity? Out of despair? Some claim that we shouldn't prepare because it would disclose evil intentions, because it would be another upward turn in the dreadful, spiraling arms race. Some claim that the building of shelters is the purest act of militarism. Well, if so, I should point to two nations in Europe, the only two in Western Europe which took shelters seriously. They are Sweden and Switzerland. If building of shelters is a sign of militarism why is it that precisely these two nations, Sweden and Switzerland, did escape the ravages of the world wars of the twentieth century?

Have I overstated the case for civil defense? Perhaps. We could indeed save 90 per cent of the people. But what do we do next? I have stated that our cities cannot be saved. What will the people do when they emerge from the shelters? Will we go back to the Stone Age? Will we starve? We need not. There has occurred a remarkable revolution in the United States that has gone almost unnoticed and about which we complain, instead of rejoicing. With a fraction of our earlier agricultural work force we have produced an embarrassing surplus of food. There are food supplies in Iowa that would be sufficient locally for half a century. In California we have food supplies only for three weeks. Furthermore, the food supplies in Iowa are stored in such a way that they may be wiped out in an attack. By the expenditure of a small amount of money we could turn the political liability of excess food into an asset, into an important measure of safety. We could distribute our food surpluses so that for two years after an attack no one need go hungry. And in those two years, if we are properly organized, we should be well on the road to recovery.

We could do much more. Instead of installing missile

defenses only for ourselves, we could install them for our allies as well. This will need nuclear explosives, but only small and clean ones over which we may exercise strict control and which can be mounted in rockets of short and controlled range. These rockets could never fall on anybody else's territory; they could be used for nothing but defense. We could give those of our allies who are in need of it enough food so that they too should be safe, and should not need to starve if they are attacked. This food would never have to enter the commercial channels and would not complicate international trade. It would be a simple measure of insuring survival in case that dreadful rainy day ever should arrive.

But all of this is not sufficient. What about our industries? You know that our country is producing each year goods in the value of five hundred billion dollars. Do you know what the value of all the goods in the country is? Prepare a long shopping list, including houses and factories, farms and minerals under the earth, food and clothing and automobiles and everything that can be bought and sold. The total value of all these goods is a thousand five hundred billion dollars—the production of three years. If enough people survive, if we stockpile the needed food, if we stockpile some of the tools so that we don't need to start the recovery process with our ten bare fingers, then in a few years we could indeed recover. And so could our allies.

In the Second World War, Germany was effectively destroyed. For three years after the end of the war there was economic chaos. Rubble was lying in the streets. The country was inert and miserable. Then, Germany introduced a stable currency, the wheels of industry slowly started to spin again and in a few more years West Germany was more wealthy than ever before. This kind of process has been repeated again and again in history. If people survive, if the elementary goods are available, then civilization is not dead. Our civilization does not reside in stone and steel but in the minds of men who understand nature and in the hearts of men who know how to cooperate with each other.

The United States is a rich country. We can afford to put into storage those goods which we need for recovery. The Russians are poor. The Chinese live on the very edge of starvation. If nuclear war should come we could survive, we could recover, and we could recover faster and more effectively than anybody else. And, contrary to popular opinion, the people who would suffer most terribly if a nuclear war would visit their country are the Chinese; because where human life hardly can be sustained, the heavy damage of a nuclear attack will become fatal.

And now I would like to complete this discussion by telling you why it is so important to work on civil defense and to build our defenses against doomsday. It is not to be prepared for an attack and even less to enable us to attack Russia. Of course, we must be prepared for an attack and we must never start a war. The real reason why civil defense is so important is this: If we are prepared, then doomsday will never come. The Communists are determined people. The men in the Kremlin have consistent, realistic plans to conquer the world. But in one respect they are very different from Hitler and his Nazis. The Russian Communists are not madmen. They are cautious. It is one of the most often quoted statements of Lenin: "I take one step backwards in order later to advance two steps." And Mao Tse-Tung, whom we call an adventurer, is quoted: "To fight against odds is not the mark of a revolutionary; it is the mark of a fool."

The Communists will never attack us if they know that we can defend ourselves. No administration of this country will initiate an attack. If we are prepared the Russians will not attack us and we shall be safe.

There is no doubt that in the world of today the preservation of peace has become most important. But in a world in which our adversaries are determined to conquer, if they can do so in a safely calculated manner—in such a world we can preserve peace only by being strong. Being strong we shall indeed preserve peace if we also are patient. If we build up our strength, if we know our strength, and if we also know the dangers of the present world, then war indeed can and will be avoided. The real danger is that we should become weak and scared. The real danger is that in our anxiety we should continue to neglect our defenses and then one day find ourselves in the desperate position where we have to admit complete defeat, where we have to acknowledge Russian supremacy, where we have to accept all of the demands of Russia or else fight. If we are weak, this day will come. If we are strong, it never needs to arrive. We have waited too long with civil defense. We were frightened for too long a period. Because this country is incredibly rich, and incredibly powerful, it is not yet too late. But in a few more years we may have lost our opportunity to save both peace and freedom.

III

THE MIRACLE OF FREEDOM

IN his book, *Science and Government,* C. P. Snow says that scientists should be consulted on matters of highest policy because they have the future in their bones. I am not sure that the predictions of scientists have been more accurate than the predictions of other people.

The majority of our scientists have not prophesied the Space Age. They have opposed it with the argument that the billions of space-dollars could better be spent on more useful or more significant scientific enterprises, like research on cancer or the exploration of the ultimate truths about physics. Scientists have not foreseen the fact that the interest of the people is powerfully attracted to the magnificent adventure of space. And I should not be surprised if the instinctive interest of the common man in the exploration of the moon would prove to be more correct and more fruitful than the conservative approach of the scientist.

Yet, in one respect I believe that the scientist can foresee the future better than the average person. We live in times of technological change. What will happen in the next decade puts the imagination of anybody to a severe test. Scientists possess at least some of the yardsticks by which tomorrow's progress should be measured. (I should not have mentioned the earthly yardstick. A telescope may be a more appropriate symbol.)

I would like to make a few predictions. We are living on a small sphere of clay and iron, and on this sphere there are some very obvious resources of which we are not yet making sufficient use—resources of the air, of the ocean, of the earth. In my first lecture I have mentioned that it ought to be possible and it will be possible to control the weather. Before the end of the century it will be possible to influence the way in which our atmosphere discharges its burden of moisture. It will be possible greatly to extend the areas which can be cultivated. And to do so it will be necessary to create some agreement between the nations of this globe.

Life has originated in the oceans. The oceans remain the greatest reservoir of life. And it is not in the dark and quiet depths where cells and algae and fish abound. It is quite close to the sunlit, wind-driven surface. We need only reach down a few feet to find food for millions. Yet we are exploiting this reservoir with the hooks and nets of our Stone-Age ancestors. We don't breed fish. We don't grow fish. We don't even know how to cultivate those meadows of algae on which the small inhabitants of the oceans can graze and in turn become the food supply for the fish population. Exploitation and control of the oceans should be possible. But it will raise problems that will not be solved by any single individual, any single company, or any single nation.

In nuclear explosives we have a concentrated form of energy which we now know how to make clean and cheap and safe. The very hydrogen bomb which first has become known because of its vast power of destruction has two significant properties. It is cheap and it can be made very clean. Because of these properties the hydrogen bomb is the best instrument for Project Plowshare, the use of nuclear explosives in the work of peace. We may cheaply move great quantities of earth and engage in geographical engineering, the building of harbors and canals. We may uncover mineral deposits beyond the range of conventional economic mining. We may deflect rivers, create lakes, and regulate the subsurface distribution of that life-giving substance—water. But the size and impact of such enterprises suggest that they may be best carried out by common effort for the benefit of more than a single nation.

There has been a great deal of justified worry about another explosion—the population explosion. But I feel confident that the earth can support ten times, thirty times its present population. Indeed, toward the end of the next century, the earth may be populated as densely as today's Greater Los Angeles. I firmly believe that the ultimate limit of the number of people is not food, not energy, not sunshine, but our ability to get along with each other. And in this sense, ethics, to which this lecture series is dedicated, is certainly the main instrument of human survival.

While we recount the helpful miracles of future technology, we must also remember that the same power that can be used in a beneficial way can be turned against our fellow citizens of this earth. The world is becoming more rich, more exciting, more remarkable, and also more dangerous. To my mind, all this adds up to one simple, unavoidable conclusion. Before the end of the twentieth century there must be established, and there will be established, law and order on an international scale, on the scale of our small world, the earth. The pace of technology, the trend of history demand this, and I firmly believe that it will be accomplished. How it will come about is another question. And this question is the subject of our discussion tonight.

At this point I must cease to speak as a scientist. Using my profession, I may make some reasonable (though fantastic) predictions about future technology. How to accomplish the political changes appropriate for the world of tomorrow is certainly not a question for which my scientific education gives me any authority. But I may still speak, though not as a scientist, but as a citizen. I should be heard not because I have studied atoms, but because I am one of the many millions of common men. My only small claim for a special hearing is this: For a quarter of a century I have lived with the knowledge that the Atomic Age will raise the great problems of rapidly increasing human power—with all the attending hopes, dangers, and responsibilities. My opinions may well be impractical. But they have been formed during many years. I may be wrong, but at least I am not capricious.

There is in the world today an expanding and frightening power—the Communist party. The facts that I have mentioned to you are, I am quite certain, completely clear to the men in the Kremlin. They know that a united world will be established in the coming decades, and they have a clear and definite plan to establish a strict world-order. They want to establish it according to the principles of their society, which principles they consider scientific. Indeed, I see ominous signs that the Communists will probably succeed in establishing their world-empire. They have an aim. They are ruthless in following that aim. They are willing to employ, in the interest of what they consider the ultimate good of mankind, every available method, including that of force and deception. In pursuing their goal, they are using the old dreadful tools of conquest, dictation, and terror. This is how powerful empires have been built in the past. It is not the first time in human history that the world, as it was known to a civilization, was united in an empire. This has happened in the time of the rulers of the Nile, for whom Egypt and later the Near East was the world. It happened in the Roman world, which extended from the burning desert to the fog-bound islands of the North. In China, the Kingdom of the Middle, the emperor claimed to rule everything between heaven and earth.

All these empires were limited only by the extent to which technology could create coherence within human society. Today technological facts cry out for the unification of the world and make such unification easy. And the Russian Communists stand ready to heed the call of history.

Let us look at ourselves. Are we ready? In 1945 the United States was considered the country to which all people of the world looked with confidence, often with gratitude and, without exception, with admiration. In 1945 it was clear that the twentieth century is the American century. What have we done in the last two decades? Our standard of living that had been the highest in the world went up by another 50 per cent. Our safety went down by more than that amount. And the respect has in many quarters turned to ridicule. There is something wrong with what we are doing. The main thing that is wrong with our way of leading the world is aimlessness. I said that the Russians do have an aim, and while I criticize their methods I have to recognize that these methods are not devoid of principle. I have to recognize that the Russian leaders are deeply convinced, as deeply as we are, that their way is the right way, the only possible way. But what do we know about their way and about the direction development in the Soviet Union is taking?

I would like to tell you about some of my experiences with Russian scientists. Those among us who say that even in Russia freedom may develop set their hopes on Russian intellectuals, primarily on Russian scientists. First of all, it is not easy to get into a political discussion with Russian visitors. They are cautious. They don't like to talk. They go around in pairs and watch each other. But when you get them into a discussion, the first thing they will assert is: "We have freedom of speech. No scientist has been sent to Siberia since Stalin died." Then I ask: "And what about discussions of politics? It's very nice that you can say about genetics, now, whatever you like; but can you criticize the Communist party line?" The answer does not come easily, but finally it does come: "You must understand. We do say generally what *Pravda* writes but don't you have to say what you read in the *Wall Street Journal*?" When anyone of us asserts that there is freedom of speech in this country on a political level, we are stared at and looked upon as either idiots or hypocrites.

It is well known to all Russians that such a thing as freedom of speech cannot really exist. It is a remarkable historical fact that the extent of Communist rule today is almost the same as the extent of the penetration of the hordes of Genghis Khan. In those countries, for almost eight hundred years, freedom of thought did not exist, freedom of conscience was a feeble glow in the ashes, freedom of discussion was stamped out. We, in our protected country, believe that freedom is a natural development. It is an exception. It is a remarkable mutation which will turn out to be not viable, if we are not careful to help it get over its dangerous decades and critical centuries. The Russians, even the technical people, even the most outstanding intellectuals, have no concept of freedom. They do have a concept of commonweal, they do have a concept of responsibility, and they consider us irresponsible. They believe that freedom is chaos.

I am firmly convinced that in a conflict like the one that exists today between Russia and the United States, between the free world and the Communist world, it won't do to underestimate our enemy; we must not underestimate his material power, nor the strength, effectiveness, and sincerity of his convictions. This, however, does not mean that we agree with him. It certainly does not mean that we predict that within the next ten or twenty years Russian Communism will have become tame.

The regimentation in Russia is as old as the Greeks, and Plato had words for it. Some of these words I have read to you. I want to read a few more now because the parallel between Socrates and Khrushchev is remarkable. This is what Socrates said (so Plato reports in the *Republic*, and he must be a good reporter) more than two thousand years ago: "The introduction of a new kind of music must be shunned as imperilling the whole state; since styles of music are never disturbed without affecting the most important political institutions."[1] New styles of music have been introduced since Socrates and, remarkable enough, these new styles have been connected with the Christian Church, an institution which is not political but religious. Music has affected in the deepest way the manner in which people live together. It was from church music that Bach developed, and if we had heeded Socrates' advice, there would be no Bach, no Mozart, no Beethoven, no Mahler, and certainly none of the modern composers. The words of Socrates sound dangerously similar to those of Khrushchev as reported in *Time* magazine, when the Russian leader gave his rather impolite lecture to the modern painters in Russia. To Khrushchev a new kind of painting does imperil the state. It is a bourgeois deviation from "peoples' art."

The Russians have a plan for world government. That plan is effective and it will subdue, govern, and perhaps even feed billions of people. Russian progress in space has shown that they have an impressive amount of initiative, and a proper amount of respect

[1]*The Republic of Plato,* Trans. John Llewelyn Davies and David James Vaughan (London: Macmillan & Co., Ltd., 1921), iii. 386.

for scientific and technical progress. But because of their history, education, and their way of thinking, they do not have any respect for the individual. They do not tolerate any change in thought, in habits, in art. Those of my friends who have visited Russia describe the Russian buildings and the Russian dinner parties as pronouncedly Victorian. It seems that under a dictatorship the habits of people are frozen. One may be willing to assume that if Russian domination should become a reality they will exercise their power without undue cruelty. But I cannot believe from all I know about the history of the world and of Russia that in the case of Russian victory, freedom of conscience, of thought, of speech will soon return to the human race. Modern technology places in the hands of the central government, of wise and regimented guardians, the ability of controlling the thoughts, the tastes, and the utterances of everyone. The guardians will regiment everyone. In such a society it takes ingenuity and courage and independence to start anything new. Ingenuity, courage, and independence are rare. The individual is all too easily crushed. Against the overwhelming weight of the state, of the laws, of the wisdom of the highest authority no man will be able to stand. I think that if the Russians win, the words of Ecclesiastes will be fulfilled. There will be nothing new under the sun.

Let us consider the chances of our own side. We live in a democracy and I have said in the first lecture that Plato did not have a high respect for the democratic government, for the democratic citizen. This is what he says about the democratic man: "burdened with expensive pleasures and desires and governed by unnecessary appetites."[2] Does that suggest to you our way of living? Well, supposedly the only way to win an election is to make sure that the standard of living should have risen by at least 3 per cent per year. Plato continues: "democracy . . . will be, in all likelihood, an agreeable, lawless, particoloured commonwealth, dealing with all alike on a footing of equality, whether they be really equal or not."[3] Does this explain to you why the rest of the world, seeing our aimless way of governing ourselves, seeing our haphazard way of helping the rest of the world, rejects our leadership? Are you surprised that under these conditions respect should indeed turn to ridicule?

And yet, there is something in our democratic tradition, in our democratic principles, of which Plato had no conception and which to my mind cannot be mentioned in the same breath with the aims of the Russian Communist party. I will not say that the Communists

---

[2] *Ibid.*, viii. 559.

[3] *Ibid.*, viii. 558.

are wicked, but I will say that Democracy can be magnificent. In each of us there is a spark, a possibility of excellence which is a high hope and an obligation. It is the democratic credo that each of us has the responsibility to find his specific way and his specific contribution to the world. It is the democratic challenge that each individual must find the star that he must follow.

I have said that the world will be under one law by the end of the century. We live in a time of incredibly fast change and there can be no doubt that history will look back at us as the genesis, as the childhood, of a new era. The face of this new world we can hardly guess, but all the great writers and the best of the psychologists have long since agreed that in the development of any individual, childhood plays a part of enormous importance.

What we do in the next few decades may change the character of the coming technological age, because the next few decades are the childhood of the new age. If in the next few decades we can change what is imperfect in democracy; if we can forget about more cars and color television sets and, instead, turn our attention to what is going on in Denmark and in Madagascar; if our tastes, which millenia ago have been rightly criticized by Socrates, should turn from the trivial to the truly interesting; and if our determination in this cold war should become comparable to the determination which we have shown in the fateful years of the early 1940's, the world may yet know and preserve freedom and the individual human soul. If not, the future will become more predictable and it will resemble much more closely that remarkable prophecy which has been linked to the year 1984.

What can one do? The Russians use the method of power, conquest, coercion. They are indeed the heirs of Genghis Khan, the greatest conquerer in human history. This ancient dishonorable art has been developed by the Communists to a new level of perfection and efficiency.

We are asking for the impossible. We want law and order, not by force but by agreement. There is no precedent in the history of the world for this kind of a change. How could we expect agreement between people basically different in tradition, in language, in their way of life, in everything that counts. We want to find a way of cooperation and equality between the yellow, the brown, the black, and the white races. We want to find a peaceful way in which feudal and tribal societies can adapt themselves to the demands of our century. We want world government by agreement, or at least we want world law. If we had a thousand years to establish it, it still would not be enough. But we have less than a century, much less. If freedom is to survive, it will be by a miracle—the miracle that millions of free and independent human beings can in fact perform. We should establish world order by the slow and safe process of evolution, but we don't have the time. It must be done by a revolution. And so I am a revolutionary, and a most reluctant one.

I remember a story that I read as a child. The author was a Swedish novelist, Selma Lagerlof. Perhaps some of you have read the adventures of Nils Holgersson, a little boy who teased animals and, as a punishment, was turned into a tiny dwarf and then carried off on the back of a goose. It was a tame goose which heard the call of the wild geese and flew away with them. The one detail which I very clearly remember is the exertion of this unhappy tame goose with little Nils Holgersson on its back, hardly able to follow the fast flight of the wild geese. She tried to catch up and cried, "Fly slower," and the wild geese returned the call, "If you fly you must fly fast." Perhaps the slow, the comfortable, the logical transition to a world order never can be executed. Perhaps the only way to fly is to fly fast.

How shall we do it? I don't know. To try to make a plan, a blueprint, is beyond human wisdom and foresight. To believe that such a plan can be written may require the confidence, perhaps the arrogance, of Plato's Guardians, whether they be philosophers, scientists, or even Communists. In our democratic world we must hope that the innumerable efforts of individuals toward the necessary goals will produce the right result.

What I shall say should not be given the dignified name of a "plan." Let me call it a proposal, a suggested first step. I do not believe that it is the best thing to do. I do not even know whether it is possible. But it may serve as an example, as a starting point of discussion, as an expression of my conviction that we must consider the problems of world law and world organization with utmost seriousness. In 1962 Nelson Rockefeller delivered the three Godkin lectures at Harvard University.[1] The first two were nice, conservative, unexciting lectures, describing the history of federalism in the United States and praising the advantages of solving local problems by local actions of the state governments, while leaving some important questions that are the concern of the Union to the federal government. The third lecture was not conservative. In this lecture Rockefeller, a man deeply

[1]Published under the title *The Future of Federalism* (Cambridge, Mass.: Harvard University Press, 1962).

rooted in the American tradition, makes the bold statement that World Communism can be stopped only by the loose and effective union of the advanced democracies, by the union of the United States with those countries that have made such wonderful progress toward a better future in that great European enterprise, the Common Market.

Indeed, the Common Market in Europe is in itself a miracle. That a few years after a devastating war the economic well-being of the European countries should have scaled new heights is good, almost incredibly good, news. But there is something that is better. And this is that progress was achieved by forgetting about old, conservative institutions; by adopting modern procedures, many of them, incidentally, imported straight from the United States. But one fact is really incredible: After the most dreadful and most unjust war waged by the Nazi government it was possible to set aside enmities which go back in history for hundreds of years. It was possible to overcome, or at least to limit, the prejudices of nationalism and work effectively, not merely toward an economic union but toward real political union. This example should encourage us that at least the first step toward an effective world order can be taken by us in the 1960's. If one decade after Hitler the French and the Germans could agree, why should it not be possible to set up a loose but effective Federal Union embracing all of the advanced free democracies?

The Federal Union of the advanced democracies can become the secure center from which freedom and abundance may spread. Of course, this cannot be anything but a mere beginning. The Industrial Revolution, with all its turbulence, with all its upsetting problems, is engulfing the whole of the earth. And whoever will be able to make sure that the Africans and the Asians and the South Americans can eat, that these people shall be saved from their present miseries, from their wretched conditions not worthy of a human being—whoever can do that, by his acts and by his examples, will be able to help to form the political ideas which will then prevail in these developing nations. And indeed, if we can set our house in order, if we can win over to the ways of freedom—to their own way of freedom—those countries that have nothing but a feudal or a tribal tradition, then, indeed, we can confront the Communists with a new situation. Because then they will not be the ones with a plan and we will no longer be floundering without aim or purpose. We shall then face them, not with a plan, but with an accomplishment which is better than any plan. Even then, it will not be easy to introduce freedom and respect for the individual in those parts of the world where these ideas never have yet taken root; even then, it will be necessary to use all our strength, all our determination and courage, and all our patience to find a peaceful and acceptable solution. But I believe that with the great experience of uniting the free, of helping the backward, we will have taken those first few strokes of the wing which will then make it possible to master the unsubstantial air around us. We might indeed become the masters of our destiny.

There is no historian who fully understands the past and there is certainly none who can predict the future. But among all these groping historians there is one contemporary writer for whom I have a deep respect. He is Arnold Toynbee. You are familiar with his theory, with his ideas of development, of sudden revolutionary heroic efforts in which men arduously try to ascend from one platform to the next, from one state of human society to a higher one. Sometimes the ascent fails; sometimes it ends in disaster. The development never takes place without a dangerous, exacting, deadly challenge. In a way we cannot complain. The challenge is here. We may fail, but I hope it will not be said about us that we have not tried.